# THE HAMILTONIAN CIRCUIT ALGORITHM

## ASHAY  DHARWADKER

# ABSTRACT

We present a new polynomial-time algorithm for finding Hamiltonian circuits in graphs. It is shown that the algorithm always finds a Hamiltonian circuit in graphs that have at least three vertices and minimum degree at least half the total number of vertices. In the process, we also obtain a constructive proof of Dirac's famous theorem of 1952, for the first time. The algorithm finds a Hamiltonian circuit (respectively, tour) in all known examples of graphs that have a Hamiltonian circuit (respectively, tour). In view of the importance of the **P** versus **NP** question, we ask: *does there exist a graph that has a Hamiltonian circuit (respectively, tour) but for which this algorithm cannot find a Hamiltonian circuit (respectively, tour)?* The algorithm is implemented in *C++* and the program is demonstrated with several examples.

*The Demonstration Program*

*http://www.dharwadker.org/hamilton*

# CONTENTS

1. INTRODUCTION           7

2. DEFINITIONS           9

3. ALGORITHM           10

4. COMPLEXITY           15

5. SUFFICIENCY           16

6. IMPLEMENTATION           18

7. PLATONIC SOLIDS           26

8. DIRAC GRAPHS           28

9. KNIGHT'S TOURS           29

10. REFERENCES           32

# 1. *Introduction*

In 1856 [1], Hamilton described a certain mathematical game called the *Icosian* played on the surface of a dodecahedron. Starting from a given vertex,

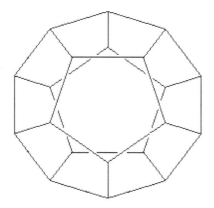

*Figure 1.1. A dodecahedron*

the objective was to find a path of consecutive vertices along the edges, visiting every vertex exactly once and returning to the original vertex to complete a circuit. The general problem of trying to find such *Hamiltonian Circuits* in arbitrary graphs turned out to be very difficult to solve.

In 1952 [2], Dirac proposed a condition that guarantees the existence of a Hamiltonian circuit in a simple graph $G$ with $n \geq 3$ vertices: *a lower bound on the minimum degree* $\delta \geq n/2$ *suffices*. This is the best possible lower bound because the graph consisting of cliques of orders $\lfloor (n + 1)/2 \rfloor$ and $\lceil (n + 1)/2 \rceil$ sharing a common vertex has minimum degree $\delta = \lfloor (n - 1)/2 \rfloor$ but has no Hamiltonian circuit. However, Dirac's original proof is a proof by contradiction that does not show how one may actually construct the stipulated Hamiltonian circuit.

In 1972 [3], Karp showed that the problem of finding Hamiltonian circuits (respectively, tours) in graphs is **NP** - complete. Thus, the existence or non-existence of a polynomial-time algorithm for deciding whether a Hamiltonian circuit (respectively, tour) exists in any given graph would resolve one of the most important open problems in mathematics and computer science, the **P** versus **NP** question [4].

This book presents A NEW ALGORITHM FOR FINDING HAMILTONIAN CIRCUITS in certain graphs. In Section 2 we provide elementary DEFINITIONS on graphs and algorithms. In Section 3 we present a formal description of the new ALGORITHM for finding Hamiltonian circuits. In Section 4 we show that the algorithm has polynomial-time COMPLEXITY. In Section 5 we present a condition of SUFFICIENCY for the algorithm to find a Hamiltonian circuit, using a lemma based on the pigeonhole principle. In the process we obtain a constructive proof of Dirac's Theorem showing, for the first time, how to build a Hamiltonian circuit in such graphs explicitly. The algorithm finds a Hamiltonian circuit (respectively, tour) in all known examples of graphs that have a Hamiltonian circuit (respectively, tour). In view of the importance of the **P** versus **NP** question, we ask: *does there exist a graph that has a Hamiltonian circuit (respectively, tour) but for which this algorithm cannot find a Hamiltonian circuit (respectively,* *tour)?* In Section 6 we provide an IMPLEMENTATION of the algorithm as a C++ program, together with demonstration software for Microsoft ™ Windows. In Section 7 we demonstrate the program for the graphs of the five PLATONIC SOLIDS, including Hamilton's original puzzle. In Section 8 we demonstrate the program for DIRAC GRAPHS which are known to be Hamiltonian. Finally, in Section 9 we further demonstrate the program by finding re-entrant KNIGHT'S TOURS on chessboards of various dimensions. Section 10 lists the REFERENCES.

# 2. *Definitions*

To begin with, we present basic definitions about graphs and algorithms following [5]. We use the usual notation $\lfloor x \rfloor$ to denote the *floor function* i.e. the greatest integer not greater than x and $\lceil x \rceil$ to denote the *ceiling function* i.e. the least integer not less than $x$.

A *simple graph G* with *n* vertices consists of a set of *vertices V*, with $|V| = n$, and a set of *edges E*, such that each edge is an unordered pair of distinct vertices. Note that the definition of *G* explicitly forbids *loops* (edges joining a vertex to itself) and *multiple edges* (many edges joining a pair of vertices), whence the set *E* must also be finite. We may *label* the vertices of *G* with the integers 1, 2, ..., *n*. If the unordered pair of vertices {*u*, *v*} is an edge in *G*, we say that *u* is a *neighbor* of *v* and write $uv \in E$. Neighborhood is clearly a symmetric relationship: $uv \in E$ if and only if $vu \in E$. The *degree* of a vertex *v*, denoted by *d*(*v*), is the number of neighbors of *v*. The *minimum degree* over all vertices of *G* is denoted by $\delta$. The *adjacency matrix* of *G* is an $n \times n$ matrix with the entry in row *u* and column *v* equal to 1 if $uv \in E$ and equal to 0 otherwise. A *path P* in *G* is a sequence of distinct vertices $v_1, v_2, ..., v_k$ such that $v_i v_{i+1} \in E$ for *i* = 1, 2, ..., *k* − 1. Given a path *P*, its sequence of distinct vertices $v_1, v_2, ..., v_k$ are said to have been *visited* and any vertex *w* outside *P* is said to be *unvisited*. Given a path *P* and a vertex *v*, the number of unvisited neighbors of *v* is denoted by $\eta(v)$. A path *P* in *G* visiting vertices $v_1, v_2, ..., v_k$ is called a *Hamiltonian tour* if *k* = *n*. Thus, a Hamiltonian tour in a simple graph is a path that visits every vertex exactly once. A path *P* in *G* visiting vertices $v_1, v_2, ..., v_n$ is called a *Hamiltonian circuit* if it is a Hamiltonian tour and $v_1 v_n \in E$. Thus, a Hamiltonian circuit in a simple graph is a path that visits every vertex exactly once and then allows us to return to the beginning of the path via an edge. If the simple graph *G* has a Hamiltonian circuit, *G* is said to be a *Hamiltonian graph*.

An *algorithm* is a problem-solving method suitable for implementation as a computer program. While designing algorithms we are typically faced with a number of different approaches. For small problems, it hardly matters which approach we use, as long as it is one that solves the problem correctly. However, there are many problems for which the only known algorithms take so long to compute the solution that they are practically useless. A *polynomial-time algorithm* is one whose number of computational steps is always bounded by a polynomial function of the size of the input. Thus, a polynomial-time algorithm is one that is actually useful in practice. The class of all such problems that have polynomial-time algorithms is denoted by **P**. For some problems, there are no known polynomial-time algorithms but these problems do have *nondeterministic polynomial-time algorithms*: try all candidates for solutions simultaneously and for each given candidate, verify whether it is a correct solution in polynomial-time. The class of all such problems is denoted by **NP**. Clearly $\mathbf{P} \subseteq \mathbf{NP}$. On the other hand, there are problems that are known to be in **NP** and are such that any polynomial-time algorithm for them can be transformed (in polynomial-time) into a polynomial-time algorithm for every problem in **NP**. Such problems are called **NP**-*complete*. The problem of finding a Hamiltonian circuit (respectively, tour) is known to be **NP**-complete [3]. Thus, if we are able to show the existence of a polynomial-time algorithm that finds a Hamiltonian circuit (respectively, tour) in every graph that has a Hamiltonian circuit (respectively, tour), we could prove that **P** = **NP**. The present algorithm is, so far as we know, a promising candidate for the task. One of the greatest unresolved problems in mathematics and computer science today is whether **P** = **NP** or **P** ≠ **NP** [4].

# 3. *Algorithm*

We are now ready to present a formal description of the algorithm. This is followed by a small example illustrating the steps of the algorithm.

**3.1. Algorithm.** Given as input a simple graph $G$ with $n$ vertices. Label the vertices $1, 2, \ldots, n$ in descending order of degrees $d(1) \geq d(2) \geq \ldots \geq d(n)$. For each initial vertex $u = 1, 2, \ldots, n$ in turn, perform Parts I, II and III as follows:

- **Part I:**
  - **Initialization:** Select the vertex $v_1 = u$ and let the path of visited vertices be $v_1$.
  - **Iteration:** Let the last selected vertex be $v_r$ and the path of visited vertices be $v_1, \ldots, v_r$. For each unvisited neighbor $w$ of $v_r$, compute $\eta(w)$, the number of unvisited neighbors of $w$. Select $v_{r+1} = w$ such that $\eta(w)$ is a minimum (if there are many possible choices, select $w$ with the smallest label). Extend the path of visited vertices to $v_1, \ldots, v_r, v_{r+1}$.
  - **Termination:** Iterate until the last selected vertex has no unvisited neighbors.
  - **Result:** A path $P^{(0)}$ visiting vertices $u = v_1, \ldots, v_k^{(0)}$ such that $v_k^{(0)}$ has no unvisited neighbors.
- **Part II:** Using the result of Part I,
  - **(a)** If $k^{(0)} < n$:
    - If there is a vertex $v_i$ in $P^{(0)}$ such that $v_i$ is a neighbor of $v_k^{(0)}$ and $v_{i+1}$ has a neighbor $w$ outside $P^{(0)}$:
      - **Initialization:** For each $v_i$ in $P^{(0)}$ such that $v_i$ is a neighbor of $v_k^{(0)}$ and $v_{i+1}$ has a neighbor $w$ outside $P^{(0)}$, and for each such neighbor $w$, compute $\eta(w)$, the number of unvisited neighbors of $w$. Choose $v_i$ and $w_0 = w$ such that $\eta(w)$ is a maximum (if there are many possible choices, choose the one where $w$ has the smallest label). Reorder the path of visited vertices to be $u = v_1, \ldots, v_{i-1}, v_i, v_k^{(0)}, v_k^{(0)}-1, \ldots, v_{i+1}$ and rename the visited vertices $u = v_1, \ldots, v_k^{(0)}$ in this order. Select the vertex $v_k^{(0)}+1 = w_0$ and let the path of visited vertices be $v_1, \ldots, v_k^{(0)}+1$. Now perform iterations exactly as in Part I to extend the path of visited vertices to $u = v_1, \ldots, v_k^{(1)}$ such that $v_k^{(1)}$ has no unvisited neighbors. Call this path $P^{(1)}$.
      - **Iteration:** Let the last computed path be $P^{(s)}$ with visited vertices $u = v_1, \ldots, v_k^{(s)}$. For each $v_i$ in $P^{(s)}$ such that $v_i$ is a neighbor of $v_k^{(s)}$ and $v_{i+1}$ has a neighbor $w$ outside $P^{(s)}$, and for each such neighbor $w$, compute $\eta(w)$, the number of unvisited neighbors of $w$. Choose $v_i$ and $w_s = w$ such that $\eta(w)$ is a maximum (if there are many possible choices, choose the one where w has the largest label). Reorder the path of visited vertices to be $u = v_1, \ldots, v_{i-1}, v_i, v_k^{(s)}, v_k^{(s)}-1, \ldots, v_{i+1}$ and rename the visited vertices $u = v_1, \ldots, v_k^{(s)}$ in this order. Select the vertex $v_k^{(s)}+1 = w_s$ and let the path of visited vertices be $v_1, \ldots, v_k^{(s)}+1$. Now perform iterations exactly as in Part I to extend the path of visited vertices to $u = v_1, \ldots, v_k^{(s+1)}$ such that $v_k^{(s+1)}$ has no unvisited neighbors. Call this path $P^{(s+1)}$.

- **Termination:** Iterate until the last selected path $P^{(s)}$ with visited vertices $u = v_1, \ldots, v_k^{(s)}$ has no vertex $v_i$ such that $v_i$ is a neighbor of $v_k^{(s)}$ and $v_{i+1}$ has a neighbor $w_s$ outside $P^{(s)}$.
  - **Result:** A path $P^{(s)}$ with visited vertices $u = v_1, \ldots, v_k^{(s)}$ such that:
    - (i) $P^{(s)}$ has no vertex $v_i$ such that $v_i$ is a neighbor of $v_k^{(s)}$ and $v_{i+1}$ has a neighbor $w_s$ outside $P^{(s)}$.
    - (ii) The vertex $v_k^{(s)}$ has no unvisited neighbors.
  - **(b)** If $k^{(s)} < n$:
    - Try to further extend the path $P^{(s)}$ by finding $v_i$ in the subpath $v_1, \ldots, v_{k^{(s)}-2}$ such that $v_i$ has a neighbor $w_1$ outside $P^{(s)}$. Now try to find a path $w_1, w_2, \ldots, w_m$ amongst the unvisited vertices by a procedure similar to Part I. Trim the path from the right, if necessary, so that $w_m$ has a neighbor $v_j$ such that $i + 1 < j < k^{(s)}$ and $v_{i+1}$ is a neighbor of $v_{j+1}$. If successful, we obtain the extended path $v_1, \ldots, v_i, w_1, w_2, \ldots, w_m, v_j, v_{j-1}, \ldots, v_{i+1}, v_{j+1}, v_{j+2}, \ldots, v_k^{(s)}$. Repeat this procedure as long as we obtain an extended path. Reassign $s$ and the extended path $P^{(s)}$ with visited vertices $u = v_1, \ldots, v_k^{(s)}$.
  - **(c)** If $k^{(s)} < n$:
    - Repeat the above procedure (b) for the reversed path $P^{(s)}$ with visited vertices $v_k^{(s)}, v_{k^{(s)}-1}, \ldots, v_1$.
- **Part III:** Using the result of Part II,
  - If $k^{(s)} < n$:
    - **Output:** Found path $v_1, \ldots, v_k^{(s)}$.
  - If $k^{(s)} = n$:
    - (i) **Output:** Found Hamiltonian tour $v_1, \ldots, v_n$.
    - (ii) Define $X = \{v_i \mid v_1 v_{i+1} \in E\}$ and $Y = \{v_i \mid v_i v_n \in E\}$. If $X \cap Y \neq \emptyset$, then for each $v_i \in X \cap Y$:
      - **Output:** Found Hamiltonian circuit $v_1, \ldots, v_{i-1}, v_i, v_n, v_{n-1}, \ldots, v_{i+1}$.
- **Exceptional Cases:**
  - **(a)** If the graph $G$ has more than two vertices of degree 1, there can be no Hamiltonian tour. If the graph $G$ has exactly two vertices of degree 1, then $G$ cannot have a Hamiltonian circuit but could have a Hamiltonian tour. Suppose the graph $G$ has exactly two vertices of degree 1, $a$ and $b$. Find a path $a = a_1, a_2, \ldots, a_r$ using the procedure of Part I such that $a_2, \ldots, a_r$ are vertices of degree 2. Similarly, find a path $b = b_1, b_2, \ldots, b_s$ such that $b_2, \ldots, b_s$ are vertices of degree 2. Now let $G_a$ be the graph obtained by deleting the vertices $a_1, a_2, \ldots, a_{r-1}, b_1, b_2, \ldots, b_s$ from $G$ and let $G_b$ be the graph obtained by deleting the vertices $a_1, a_2, \ldots, a_r, b_1, b_2, \ldots, b_{s-1}$ from $G$. Use Parts I and II to find paths in the graphs $G_a$ and $G_b$. If a path in $G_a$ can be connected to a path in $G_b$ to form a path in $G$, use Parts I and II to try and extend such a path to a Hamiltonian tour in $G$.
  - **(b)** Suppose the algorithm finds a Hamiltonian tour in $G$ but Part III could not find a Hamiltonian circuit. For each edge $ab$ in $G$, let $G_{ab}$ denote the graph obtained by deleting the edge $ab$ in $G$ and adding two new vertices $a'$ and $b'$ and two new edges $aa'$ and $bb'$. Use the algorithm to try and find a Hamiltonian tour $a', a, \ldots, b, b'$ in $G_{ab}$. Then $a, \ldots, b$ would be a Hamiltonian circuit in $G$.

11

**3.2. Example.** We demonstrate some of the steps of the algorithm with a small example. Consider the labeled graph with $n = 8$ vertices shown below in Figure 3.1. We go through the steps for initial vertex $u = 1$.

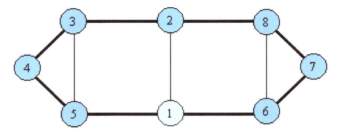

*Figure 3.1. A small example to demonstrate the steps of the algorithm*

First perform Part I. To initialize (Iteration 1), we select $v_1 = 1$ and let the path of visited vertices be $v_1 = 1$. The unvisited neighbors of $v_1 = 1$ are 2, 5 and 6. The vertex 2 has two unvisited neighbors 3 and 8, so $\eta(2) = 2$; the vertex 5 has two unvisited neighbors 3 and 4, so $\eta(5) = 2$; the vertex 6 has two unvisited neighbors 7 and 8, so $\eta(6) = 2$. Here vertex 2 has the smallest label such that $\eta(2) = 2$ is a minimum. At Iteration 2, select $v_2 = 2$ and let the path of visited vertices be $v_1 = 1$, $v_2 = 2$. The unvisited neighbors of $v_2 = 2$ are 3 and 8. The vertex 3 has two unvisited neighbors 4 and 5, so $\eta(3) = 2$; the vertex 8 has two unvisited neighbors 6 and 7, so $\eta(8) = 2$. Here vertex 3 has the smallest label such that $\eta(3) = 2$ is a minimum. At Iteration 3, select $v_3 = 3$ and let the path of visited vertices be $v_1 = 1$, $v_2 = 2$, $v_3 = 3$. The unvisited neighbors of $v_3 = 3$ are 4 and 5. The vertex 4 has only one unvisited neighbor 5, so $\eta(4) = 1$; the vertex 5 also has only one unvisited neighbor 4, so $\eta(5) = 1$. Here vertex 4 has the smallest label such that $\eta(4) = 1$ is a minimum. At Iteration 4, select $v_4 = 4$ and let the path of visited vertices be $v_1 = 1$, $v_2 = 2$, $v_3 = 3$, $v_4 = 4$. The only unvisited neighbor of $v_4 = 4$ is 5. The vertex 5 has no unvisited neighbors, so $\eta(5) = 0$. We select $v_5 = 5$, and let the path of visited vertices be $v_1 = 1$, $v_2 = 2$, $v_3 = 3$, $v_4 = 4$, $v_5 = 5$. Part I terminates with the resulting path $P^{(0)}$ visiting vertices $v_1 = 1$, $v_2 = 2$, $v_3 = 3$, $v_4 = 4$, $v_5 = 5$ and cardinality $k^{(0)} = 5$.

Now perform Part II. We have $k^{(0)} = 5 < 8 = n$. The neighbors of $v_5 = 5$ are $v_1 = 1$, $v_3 = 3$ and $v_4 = 4$, all in $P^{(0)}$ by construction. Consider the respective successor vertices $v_{1+1} = v_2 = 2$, $v_{3+1} = v_4 = 4$ and $v_{4+1} = v_5 = 5$. Now $v_2 = 2$ has only one neighbor 8 outside $P^{(0)}$. The vertex 8 has two unvisited neighbors 6 and 7, so $\eta(8) = 2$. The vertices $v_4 = 4$ and $v_5 = 5$ have no neighbors outside $P^{(0)}$ to consider. Here $v_1 = 1$ (trivially, with no comparisons to be made) has the largest label such that its successor $v_{1+1} = v_2 = 2$ has a neighbor 8 outside $P^{(0)}$ with maximum $\eta(8) = 2$. We first reorder the path of visited vertices $v_1 = 1$, $v_5 = 5$, $v_4 = 4$, $v_3 = 3$, $v_2 = 2$. We then rename the path of visited vertices in this order $v_1 = 1$, $v_2 = 5$, $v_3 = 4$, $v_4 = 3$, $v_5 = 2$. Now select the vertex $v_6 = 8$ found above and let the path of visited vertices be $v_1 = 1$, $v_2 = 5$, $v_3 = 4$, $v_4 = 3$, $v_5 = 2$, $v_6 = 8$. Perform iterations exactly as in Part I from here: the unvisited neighbors of $v_6 = 8$ are 6 and 7. The vertex 6 has only one unvisited neighbor 7, so $\eta(6) = 1$; the vertex 7 also has only one unvisited neighbor 6, so $\eta(7) = 1$. Here vertex 6 has the smallest label such that $\eta(6) = 1$ is a minimum. At the next iteration, select $v_7 = 6$ and let the path of visited vertices be $v_1 = 1$, $v_2 = 5$, $v_3 = 4$, $v_4 = 3$, $v_5 = 2$, $v_6 = 8$, $v_7 = 6$. The only unvisited neighbor of $v_7 = 6$ is 7. The vertex 7 has

12

no unvisited neighbors, so $\eta$ (7) = 0. We select $v_8 = 7$ and obtain the path $P^{(1)}$ with visited vertices $v_1 = 1$, $v_2 = 5$, $v_3 = 4$, $v_4 = 3$, $v_5 = 2$, $v_6 = 8$, $v_7 = 6$, $v_8 = 7$. Since there are no vertices left outside $P^{(1)}$, Part II terminates with the resulting path $P^{(1)}$ visiting vertices $v_1 = 1$, $v_2 = 5$, $v_3 = 4$, $v_4 = 3$, $v_5 = 2$, $v_6 = 8$, $v_7 = 6$, $v_8 = 7$ and cardinality $k^{(1)} = 8$.

Finally, perform Part III. Since $k^{(1)} = 8 = n$, the algorithm has found a Hamiltonian tour. Define $X = \{v_i \mid v_1 v_{i+1} \in E\} = \{v_1, v_4, v_6\} = \{1, 3, 8\}$ and $Y = \{v_i \mid v_i v_n \in E\} = \{v_6, v_7\} = \{8, 6\}$. Then $X \cap Y = \{v_6\} = \{8\}$, so the algorithm has found a Hamiltonian circuit $v_1 = 1$, $v_2 = 5$, $v_3 = 4$, $v_4 = 3$, $v_5 = 2$, $v_6 = 8$, $v_8 = 7$, $v_7 = 6$.

Similarly, we can go through Parts I, II and III starting with initial vertices $u = 2, 3, 4, 5, 6, 7$ and 8 respectively.

**3.3. Example.** Provided by Guenter Stertenbrink, February 2005 [Download]. This example shows that it is necessary to order the vertices by descending degrees and Parts II(b) and II(c) are also used.

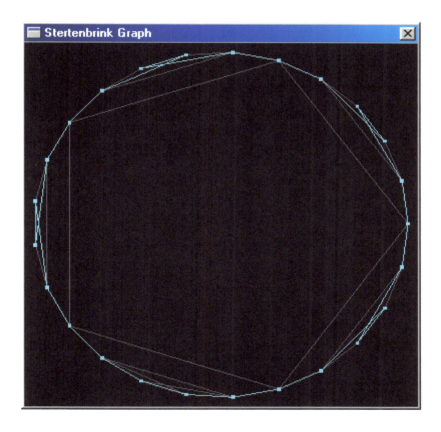

***Figure 3.2.*** *The algorithm finds a Hamiltonian circuit in Stertenbrink's graph*

**3.4. Example.** Provided by Roberto Tauraso, November 2005 [Download]. This example shows how the algorithm works in the exceptional cases (a) and (b).

*Figure 3.2.* *The algorithm finds a Hamiltonian circuit in Tauraso's graph*

A *square loop* of size $n$ is a circular arrangement of the integers 1, 2, …, $n$ such that the sum of any two adjacent integers is a perfect square. Define a graph $G_n$ with vertices 1, 2, …, $n$ such that there is an edge between vertex $i$ and vertex $j$ if and only if $i + j$ is a perfect square. Then a Hamiltonian circuit in $G_n$ is exactly a square loop of size $n$. The graph of figure 3.2 shows a Hamiltonian circuit in $G_{32}$ and a square loop of size 32. Roberto Tauraso and his students computed many large square loops using this algorithm and conjecture that square loops exist for all $n \geq 32$.

# 4. *Complexity*

We shall now show that the above algorithm terminates in polynomial-time, by specifying a polynomial of the number of vertices $n$ of the input graph, that is an upper bound on the total number of computational steps performed by the algorithm. Note that we consider
- checking whether a given pair of vertices is connected by an edge in $G$, and
- comparing whether a given integer is less than another given integer

to be *elementary computational steps*.

**4.1. Proposition.** *Given as input a simple graph $G$ with $n$ vertices, the algorithm takes less than $4n^5 + 8n^4 + 3n^3 + 2n^2 + n$ steps to terminate.*

*Proof.* Given an initial vertex $u$, first consider Part I of the algorithm. At iteration $r$, it takes less than $n$ steps to determine the unvisited neighbors $v^{(r)}_1, \ldots, v^{(r)}_m$ of $v_r$. Then for each $v^{(r)}_i$ it takes less than $n$ steps to determine the unvisited neighbors of $v^{(r)}_i$ and hence find $\eta(v^{(r)}_i)$. Thereafter it takes less than $n$ steps to find the minimum of the integers $\eta(v^{(r)}_1), \ldots, \eta(v^{(r)}_m)$. Thus we count a total of less than $n^2 + n$ steps at iteration $r$. There are at most $n$ iterations, so a total of less than $n(n^2 + n) = n^3 + n^2$ steps terminates Part I to find path $P^{(0)}$.

Next consider Part II. If $k^{(0)} < n$, it takes less than $n$ steps to determine the neighbors of $v_k^{(0)}$. Thereafter, it takes less than $n$ steps to try and find a neighbor $w$ outside $P^{(0)}$ for each successor of a neighbor of $v_k^{(0)}$. For each such neighbor $w$, it takes less than $n$ steps to count its $\eta(w)$ unvisited neighbors. So it takes less than $n^3$ steps to find all the $\eta(w)$ and then it takes less than $n$ steps to find $w$ for which $\eta(w)$ is a maximum. Thus we count less than $n^3 + n$ steps so far in Part II (a). Now reordering and renaming the vertices takes less than $n$ steps, and then the iterations to find path $P^{(1)}$ take less than $n^3 + n^2$ steps, exactly as in Part I. Thus we count less than $n^3 + n + n + n^3 + n^2 = 2n^3 + n^2 + 2n$ steps so far in Part II (a). Since Part II performs at most $n$ iterations, a total of less than $n(2n^3 + n^2 + 2n) = 2n^4 + n^3 + 2n^2$ steps terminates Part II (a) to find path $P^{(s)}$. If Part II (b) is required, it takes less than $n^2$ steps to find $v_i$ and $w_1$. Thereafter, it takes less than $n^3 + n^2$ steps as in Part I to find the path $w_1, w_2, \ldots, w_m$ and less than $n^2$ steps to find $v_j$. Since there can be at most $n$ iterations, Part II(b) takes less than $n(n^2 + n^3 + n^2 + n^2) = n^4 + 3n^3$ steps. Similarly, Part II (c) takes less than $n^4 + 3n^3$ steps. Thus Part II takes less than $2n^4 + n^3 + 2n^2 + n^4 + 3n^3 + n^4 + 3n^3 = 4n^4 + 7n^3 + 2n^2$ steps to terminate.

Finally consider Part III. Here (i) is just one step and (ii) may be accomplished in less than $2n$ steps, thus a total of less than $2n + 1$ steps terminates Part III.

Hence, the algorithm starting at any initial vertex $u$, takes a total of less than $n^3 + n^2 + 4n^4 + 7n^3 + 2n^2 + 2n + 1 = 4n^4 + 8n^3 + 3n^2 + 2n + 1$ steps to complete Parts I, II and III. Since there are $n$ choices for the initial vertex, the algorithm must finally terminate after executing a grand total of less than $n(4n^4 + 8n^3 + 3n^2 + 2n + 1) = 4n^5 + 8n^4 + 3n^3 + 2n^2 + n$ steps. ∎

**4.2. Remark.** A simple graph $G$ with $n$ vertices can have at most $n(n-1)/2$ edges. In the exceptional case (b), the algorithm will run once for each edge, so the running time of the program will increase at most by a factor of $\mathbf{O}(n^2)$.

# 5. *Sufficiency*

The algorithm may be applied to any simple graph and will always terminate in polynomial-time. The theorem below establishes a sufficient condition on the input graph which guarantees that the algorithm will find a Hamiltonian circuit. As a corollary we obtain a constructive proof of Dirac's theorem [2]. For the proof of the theorem, we shall need the following lemma that is a direct consequence of the

**5.1. Pigeonhole Principle.** If $l$ letters are distributed into $p$ pigeonholes and $l > p \geq 1$, then some pigeonhole must receive at least two letters.

**5.2. Lemma.** *Let $G$ be a simple graph with $n \geq 3$ vertices and $\delta \geq n/2$. If $X$ is a subset with $\lceil n/2 \rceil$ vertices and $v$ is a vertex outside $X$ then $v$ must have a neighbor in $X$.*

*Proof.* If $n = 3$, $X$ must consist of the two vertices other than $v$ and since $d(v) \geq 2$ both vertices in $X$ must be neighbors of $v$. Let $n > 3$ and suppose $v$ has no neighbors in $X$. Then since $d(v) \geq n/2$, there are at least $l = \lceil n/2 \rceil$ edges (letters) with one end vertex $v$ and the other end vertex among the $p = n - 1 - \lceil n/2 \rceil \geq 1$ vertices (pigeonholes) excluding $v$ and $X$. Since $l > p$, the pigeonhole principle implies that some pigeonhole vertex must receive at least two edges with the other end vertex being $v$. This contradicts the fact that $G$ is simple and has no multiple edges. Thus $v$ must have a neighbor in $X$. ∎

**5.3. Theorem.** *If $G$ is a simple graph with $n \geq 3$ vertices and $\delta \geq n/2$, then the algorithm finds a Hamiltonian circuit in $G$.*

*Proof.* Label the vertices of the graph $G$ as $1, 2, \ldots, n$. Start at any initial vertex $u$. We first show that the path $P^{(0)}$ produced by Part I contains more than $\lceil n/2 \rceil$ vertices. Consider the iterations of Part I.

Iteration 1 (Initialization): We select vertex $v_1 = u$ and initialize the path of visited vertices to be $v_1$. Using the hypothesis $\delta \geq n/2$, there are at least $\lceil n/2 \rceil$ unvisited neighbors of $v_1$ and for each unvisited neighbor $w$ of $v_1$ we have $\eta(w) \geq \lceil n/2 \rceil - 1$, since there is only one visited vertex so far. Let $v_2 = w$ be the unvisited neighbor of $v_1$ with the smallest label such that $\eta(w)$ is a minimum.

Iteration 2: We select vertex $v_2$ and update the path of visited vertices to be $v_1, v_2$. Using the hypothesis $\delta \geq n/2$, there are at least $\lceil n/2 \rceil - 1$ unvisited neighbors of $v_2$ and for each unvisited neighbor $w$ of $v_2$ we have $\eta(w) \geq \lceil n/2 \rceil - 2$, since there are only two visited veeertices so far. Let $v_3 = w$ be the unvisited neighbor of $v_2$ with the smallest label such that $\eta(w)$ is a minimum.

Continuing to iterate this way without termination, we arrive at:

Iteration $\lceil n/2 \rceil$: We select vertex $v_{\lceil n/2 \rceil}$ and update the path of visited vertices to be $v_1, v_2, \ldots, v_{\lceil n/2 \rceil}$. Using the hypothesis $\delta \geq n/2$, there is at least $\lceil n/2 \rceil - (\lceil n/2 \rceil - 1) = 1$ unvisited neighbor $w$ of $v_{\lceil n/2 \rceil}$ and for each unvisited neighbor $w$ of $v_{\lceil n/2 \rceil}$ we have $\eta(w) \geq \lceil n/2 \rceil - \lceil n/2 \rceil = 0$, since there are only $\lceil n/2 \rceil$ visited vertices so far. Let $v_{\lceil n/2 \rceil + 1} = w$ be the unvisited neighbor of $v_{\lceil n/2 \rceil}$ with the smallest label such that $\eta(w)$ is a minimum.

We must finally arrive at Iteration $k^{(0)}$ where we select a vertex $v_k^{(0)}$ such that $v_k^{(0)}$ has no unvisited neighbors and then Part I terminates. Thus, as a result of Part I, we have a path $P^{(0)}$ with vertices $u = v_1, \ldots, v_k^{(0)}$ such that all the neighbors of $v_k^{(0)}$ are in $P^{(0)}$ and $k^{(0)} > \lceil n/2 \rceil$.

We now show that the path $P^{(s)}$ produced by Part II must be a Hamiltonian tour with $k^{(s)} = n$. If $k^{(0)} = n$, we are done. Suppose $k^{(0)} < n$, so that there exists a vertex $w$ outside the path $P^{(0)}$. Note that by construction $v_k^{(0)}$ has at least $\lceil n/2 \rceil$ neighbors in $P^{(0)}$, say $v_t^{(1)}, v_t^{(2)}, \ldots, v_t^{(\lceil n/2 \rceil)}$. Using the Lemma, any such $w$ must have a neighbor amongst the $\lceil n/2 \rceil$ distinct vertices $v_t^{(1)}+1$, $v_t^{(2)}+1, \ldots, v_t^{(\lceil n/2 \rceil)}+1$ in $P^{(0)}$. Then the initialization of Part II chooses a $v_t^{(i)}$ and a $w_0$ with maximal $\eta(w_0)$ to produce a path $P^{(1)}$ with reordered and renamed vertices $u = v_1, \ldots, v_k^{(1)}$ that contains all the vertices of $P^{(0)}$ plus the vertex $w_0$. If $k^{(1)} = n$, we are done. Again, suppose $k^{(1)} < n$, so that there exists a vertex $w$ outside the path $P^{(1)}$. Note that by construction $v_k^{(1)}$ has at least $\lceil n/2 \rceil$ neighbors in $P^{(1)}$, say $v_t^{(1)}, v_t^{(2)}, \ldots, v_t^{(\lceil n/2 \rceil)}$. Using the Lemma, any such $w$ must have a neighbor amongst the $\lceil n/2 \rceil$ distinct vertices $v_t^{(1)}+1, v_t^{(2)}+1, \ldots, v_t^{(\lceil n/2 \rceil)}+1$ in $P^{(1)}$. Then the iteration of Part II chooses a $v_t^{(i)}$ and a $w_1$ with maximal $\eta(w_1)$ to produce a path $P^{(2)}$ with reordered and renamed vertices $u = v_1, \ldots, v_k^{(2)}$ that contains all the vertices of $P^{(1)}$ plus the vertex $w_1$. Repeating the same argument, as long as there is a vertex outside the path $P^{(i)}$, the iterations of Part II will continue to produce extended paths $P^{(i+1)}$ such that $P^{(i+1)}$ starts at $u$, contains all the vertices of $P^{(i)}$ (in some order) plus a vertex $w_i$ that was outside the path $P^{(i)}$. Since there are only finitely many vertices, Part II must finally terminate resulting in a path $P^{(s)}$ with visited vertices $u = v_1, \ldots, v_k^{(s)}$ such that $k^{(s)} = n$. Hence the algorithm, starting at any initial vertex $u$, always produces a Hamiltonian tour $P^{(s)}$ with vertices $u = v_1, \ldots, v_n$ as a result of Part II.

To complete the proof, we show that Part III constructs a Hamiltonian circuit from the Hamiltonian tour $P^{(s)}$. Since $k^{(s)} = n$, in Part III (ii), the algorithm defines $X = \{v_i \mid v_1 v_{i+1} \in E\}$ and $Y = \{v_i \mid v_i v_n \in E\}$. If $v_1 v_n \in E$, then since $v_{n-1} v_n \in E$ by the definition of $P^{(s)}$, we have $v_{n-1} \in X \cap Y$ and the algorithm has found the Hamiltonian circuit $v_1, \ldots, v_{n-1}, v_n$. On the other hand, if $v_1 v_n \notin E$, then we claim that $X \cap Y \neq \varnothing$, as follows. Since $v_n \notin X \cup Y$ we have $|X \cup Y| < n$ and if $|X \cap Y| = 0$ then $d(v_1) + d(v_n) = |X| + |Y| = |X \cup Y| + |X \cap Y| < n$, contradicting the hypothesis $\delta \geq n/2$. Hence there exists $v_i \in X \cap Y$ and the algorithm has found the Hamiltonian circuit $v_1, \ldots, v_{i-1}, v_i, v_n, v_{n-1}, \ldots, v_{i+1}$. ∎

**5.4. Corollary.** (Dirac 1952, [2]). *As an immediate consequence of the theorem, if G is a simple graph with $n \geq 3$ vertices and $\delta \geq n/2$, then G is Hamiltonian.*

**5.5. Question.** Let $G$ be a simple graph with $n$ vertices. The theorem shows that Dirac's conditions $n \geq 3$ and $\delta \geq n/2$ are sufficient for the algorithm to find a Hamiltonian circuit in $G$. Examples 3, the Platonic graphs in section 7 and the re-entrant knight's tours in section 8 show that Dirac's conditions are not necessary for the algorithm to find a Hamiltonian circuit in $G$. All the known examples show that whenever a graph $G$ has a Hamiltonian circuit (respectively, tour), the algorithm finds a Hamiltonian circuit (respectively, tour) in $G$.

- *Does there exist a graph G that has a Hamiltonian circuit (respectively, tour) but for which the algorithm cannot find any Hamiltonian circuit (respectively, tour)?*

Since the problem of determining whether a simple graph has a Hamiltonian circuit (respectively, tour) is known to be **NP – complete** [3], and our algorithm is polynomial-time by the proposition, a negative answer to the question would imply **P = NP**.

# 6.  *Implementation*

We provide a *C++* program, *hamilton.cpp*, in the style of [6], that implements the algorithm, together with sample input/output files.

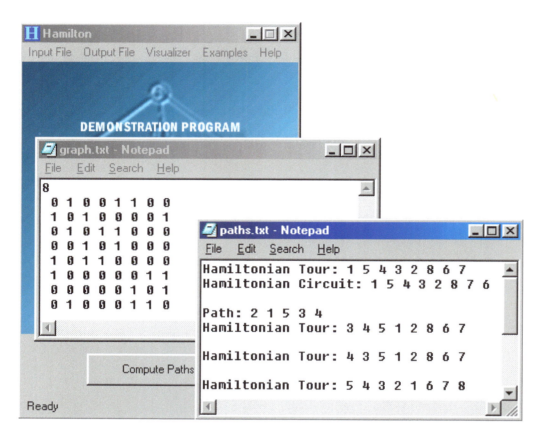

**Figure 6.1.** *Demonstration Program for Windows* [Download]

**6.1. Program.** The following program will make a simple console application, and is included in the Demonstration Program package. The program was tested using Microsoft ™ Visual C++ 6.0.

```cpp
#include <iostream>
#include <fstream>
#include <string>
#include <vector>
using namespace std;
vector<int> procedure_1(vector< vector<int> > graph, vector<int> path);
vector<int> procedure_2(vector< vector<int> > graph, vector<int> path);
vector<int> procedure_2b(vector< vector<int> > graph, vector<int> path);
vector<int> procedure_2c(vector< vector<int> > graph, vector<int> path);
vector<int> procedure_3(vector< vector<int> > graph, vector<int> path);
vector<int> sort(vector<vector<int> > graph);
vector<vector<int> >
```

18

```cpp
          reindex(vector<vector<int> > graph, vector<int> index);
ifstream infile ("graph.txt");        //Input file
ofstream outfile("paths.txt");        //Output file

int main()
{
 int i, j, k, n, vertex, edge;
 infile>>n;                            //Read number of vertices
 vector< vector<int> > graph;          //Read adjacency matrix of graph
 for(i=0; i<n; i++)
 {
  vector<int> row;
  for(j=0; j<n; j++)
  {
   infile>>edge;
   row.push_back(edge);
  }
  graph.push_back(row);
 }

 vector<int> index=sort(graph);
 graph=reindex(graph,index);

 for(vertex=0; vertex<n; vertex++)   //Loop through all vertices
 {
  vector<int> path;
  path.push_back(vertex);               //Select initial vertex
  path=procedure_1(graph,path);        //Part I
  path=procedure_2(graph,path);        //Part II
  k=path.size();
  if(k<n)    {path=procedure_2b(graph,path); k=path.size();}
  if(k<n)    {path=procedure_2c(graph,path); k=path.size();}
  if(k<n) outfile<<"Path("<<k<<"): ";
  else outfile<<"Hamiltonian Tour: ";//Part III
  for(i=0; i<path.size(); i++) outfile<<index[path[i]]+1<<" ";
  outfile<<endl;
  if(k==n)
  {
   vector<int> circuit_maker=procedure_3(graph,path);
   if(!circuit_maker.empty())
   {
    for(j=0; j<circuit_maker.size(); j++)
    {
     outfile<<"Hamiltonian Circuit:\t";
     for(k=0; k<=circuit_maker[j]; k++)
      outfile<<index[path[k]]+1<<" ";
     for(k=n-1; k>circuit_maker[j]; k--)
      outfile<<index[path[k]]+1<<" ";
     outfile<<endl;
    }
   }
   outfile<<endl;
  }
 }
 cout<<"See paths.txt for results."<<endl;
  system("PAUSE");
  return 0;
```

```cpp
}

vector<int> procedure_1(vector< vector<int> > graph, vector<int> path)
{
 int i, j, k, n=graph.size();
 vector<int> extended_path;
 vector<int> visited;
 for(i=0; i<n; i++)
  visited.push_back(0);
 int present;
 for(i=0; i<path.size(); i++)
 {
  present=path[i];
  visited[present]=1;
  extended_path.push_back(present);
 }
 for(k=0; k<n; k++)
 {
  vector<int> neighbor;
  for(i=0; i<n; i++)
   if(graph[present][i]==1 && visited[i]==0)
    neighbor.push_back(i);
   if(!neighbor.empty())
   {
    int choice=neighbor[0];
    int minimum=n;
    for(i=0; i<neighbor.size(); i++)
    {
     vector<int> next_neighbor;
     for(j=0; j<n; j++)
      if(graph[neighbor[i]][j]==1 && visited[j]==0)
       next_neighbor.push_back(j);
      int eta=next_neighbor.size();
      if(eta<minimum)
      {
       choice=neighbor[i];
       minimum=eta;
      }
    }
    present=choice;
    visited[present]=1;
    extended_path.push_back(present);
   }
   else break;
 }
 return extended_path;
}

vector<int> procedure_2(vector< vector<int> > graph, vector<int> path)
{
 int i, j, k, n=graph.size();
 bool quit=false;
 while(quit!=true)
 {
 int m=path.size(), inlet=-1, outlet=-1;
  vector<int> neighbor;
```

```
  for(i=0; i<path.size(); i++)
   if(graph[path[m-1]][path[i]]==1) neighbor.push_back(i);
   vector<int> unvisited;
   for(i=0; i<n; i++)
    {
     bool outside=true;
     for(j=0; j<path.size(); j++)
      if(i==path[j]) outside=false;
      if(outside==true) unvisited.push_back(i);
    }
   if((!unvisited.empty()) && (!neighbor.empty()))
    {
     int maximum=0;
     for(i=0; i<neighbor.size(); i++)
      for(j=0; j<unvisited.size(); j++)
       if(graph[path[neighbor[i]+1]][unvisited[j]]==1)
        {
         vector<int> next_neighbor;
         for(k=0; k<unvisited.size(); k++)
          if(graph[unvisited[j]][unvisited[k]]==1)
           next_neighbor.push_back(unvisited[k]);
          int eta=next_neighbor.size();
          if(eta>=maximum)
           {
            inlet=neighbor[i];
            outlet=unvisited[j];
            maximum=eta;
           }
        }
    }
   vector<int> extended_path;
   if(inlet!=-1 && outlet!=-1)
    {
     for(i=0; i<=inlet; i++)
      extended_path.push_back(path[i]);
     for(i=path.size()-1; i>inlet; i--)
      extended_path.push_back(path[i]);
     extended_path.push_back(outlet);
    }
   if(!extended_path.empty()) path=extended_path;
   if(m<path.size()) path=procedure_1(graph,path);
   else quit=true;
 }
 return path;
}

vector<int> procedure_2b(vector< vector<int> > graph, vector<int> path)
{
 int i, j, k, l, p, n=graph.size();
 bool quit=false;
 while(quit!=true)
 {
  vector<int> extended_path;
  int m=path.size();
  vector<int> unvisited;
  for(i=0; i<n; i++)
   {
```

```cpp
      bool outside=true;
      for(j=0; j<path.size(); j++)
       if(i==path[j]) outside=false;
      if(outside==true) unvisited.push_back(i);
   }
   bool big_check=false;
   for(i=0; i<path.size(); i++)
   {
      for(j=0; j<unvisited.size(); j++)
      {
       if(graph[unvisited[j]][path[i]]==1)
       {
         vector<int> temp_path;
         temp_path.push_back(unvisited[j]);
         vector<int> temp_extended_path;
         vector<int> temp_visited;
         for(l=0; l<n; l++)
         temp_visited.push_back(0);
         int present;
         for(l=0; l<temp_path.size(); l++)
         {
          present=temp_path[l];
          temp_visited[present]=1;
          temp_extended_path.push_back(present);
         }
         for(l=0; l<n; l++)
         {
          bool unfound=true;
          for(k=0; k<unvisited.size(); k++)
           if(l==unvisited[k]) unfound=false;
          if(unfound==true) temp_visited[l]=1;
         }
         for(l=0; l<n; l++)
         {
          vector<int> neighbor;
          for(l=0; l<n; l++)
          if(graph[present][l]==1 && temp_visited[l]==0)
          neighbor.push_back(l);
          if(!neighbor.empty())
          {
            int choice=neighbor[0];
            int minimum=n;
            for(l=0; l<neighbor.size(); l++)
            {
             vector<int> next_neighbor;
             for(k=0; k<n; k++)
              if(graph[neighbor[l]][k]==1 && temp_visited[k]==0)
              next_neighbor.push_back(k);
              int eta=next_neighbor.size();
              if(eta<minimum)
              {
               choice=neighbor[l];
               minimum=eta;
              }
            }
           present=choice;
           temp_visited[present]=1;
```

```
            temp_extended_path.push_back(present);
        }
      else break;
    }
    int last_vertex=temp_extended_path[temp_extended_path.size()-1];
    int vj;
    bool check=false;
    while(check==false && !temp_extended_path.empty())
    {
    for(p=path.size()-2; p>i; p--)
    {
     if(graph[path[p]][last_vertex]==1
        && graph[path[i+1]][path[p+1]]==1)
     {
      check=true;
      vj=p;
      break;
     }
    }
    if(check==false)
    {
     temp_extended_path.pop_back();
     last_vertex=temp_extended_path[temp_extended_path.size()-1];
    }
    }
    if(check==true)
    {
     vector<int> temp;
     for(p=0; p<=i; p++)
     temp.push_back(path[p]);
     for(p=0; p<temp_extended_path.size(); p++)
     temp.push_back(temp_extended_path[p]);
     for(p=vj; p>i; p--)
     temp.push_back(path[p]);
     for(p=vj+1; p<path.size(); p++)
     temp.push_back(path[p]);
     temp_extended_path=temp;
     big_check=true;
     extended_path=temp_extended_path;
    }
    }
    }
     if(big_check==true)
     {
      break;
     }
  }
  if(!extended_path.empty()) path=extended_path;
  if(m<path.size())
  {
   path=procedure_1(graph,path);
   path=procedure_2(graph,path);
  }
  else quit=true;
 }
 return path;
}
```

```cpp
vector<int> procedure_2c(vector< vector<int> > graph, vector<int> path)
{
  vector<int> reversed_path;
  for(int i=path.size()-1; i>=0; i--) reversed_path.push_back(path[i]);
  reversed_path=procedure_2b(graph,reversed_path);
  return reversed_path;
}

vector<int> procedure_3(vector< vector<int> > graph, vector<int> path)
{

 int i, n=path.size();

 vector<int> circuit_maker;
 for(i=0; i<n-1; i++)
  if((graph[path[0]][path[i+1]]==1) && (graph[path[i]][path[n-1]]==1))
    circuit_maker.push_back(i);
 return circuit_maker;
}

vector<int> sort(vector<vector<int> > graph)
{
 int i, j;
 vector<int> degree;
 for(i=0; i<graph.size(); i++)
 {
  int sum=0;
  for(j=0; j<graph[i].size(); j++)
  if(graph[i][j]==1) sum++;
  degree.push_back(sum);
 }
 vector<int> index;
 for(i=0; i<degree.size(); i++) index.push_back(i);
 for(i=0; i<degree.size(); i++)
 for(j=i+1; j<degree.size(); j++)
 if(degree[i]<degree[j]) swap(index[i],index[j]);
 return index;
}

vector<vector<int> >
      reindex(vector<vector<int> > graph, vector<int> index)
{
  int i, j;
  vector<vector<int> > temp=graph;
  for(i=0; i<temp.size(); i++)
  for(j=0; j<temp[i].size(); j++)
  temp[i][j]=graph[index[i]][index[j]];
  return temp;
}
```

**6.2. Input File.** The input file for the program, *graph.txt*, has as first entry the number of vertices of the graph, followed by white space, followed by the entries of the adjacency matrix of the graph in row-major order, all separated by white space. We use the graph of Example 3.2.

```
                8
        0 1 0 0 1 1 0 0
        1 0 1 0 0 0 0 1
        0 1 0 1 1 0 0 0
        0 0 1 0 1 0 0 0
        1 0 1 1 0 0 0 0
        1 0 0 0 0 0 1 1
        0 0 0 0 0 1 0 1
        0 1 0 0 0 1 1 0
```

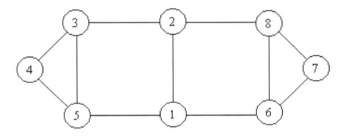

**6.3. Output File.** The output file for the program, *paths.txt*, lists the paths, tours and circuits found by the algorithm.

```
paths.txt
Hamiltonian Tour: 1 5 4 3 2 8 6 7
Hamiltonian Circuit: 1 5 4 3 2 8 7 6
Path: 2 1 5 3 4
Hamiltonian Tour: 3 4 5 1 2 8 6 7
Hamiltonian Tour: 4 3 5 1 2 8 6 7
Hamiltonian Tour: 5 4 3 2 1 6 7 8
Hamiltonian Circuit: 5 4 3 2 8 7 6 1
Hamiltonian Tour: 6 7 8 2 1 5 3 4
Hamiltonian Tour: 7 6 8 2 1 5 3 4
Hamiltonian Tour: 8 7 6 1 2 3 4 5
Hamiltonian Circuit: 8 7 6 1 5 4 3 2
```

# 7.   *Platonic Solids*

Convex polyhedra with faces composed of congruent convex regular polygons are called *Platonic solids*. In the last Book of the Elements, Euclid [9] proved that there are exactly five platonic solids as described by Plato [10]: the tetrahedron, the octahedron, the cube, the icosahedron and the dodecahedron. The graphs consisting of vertices and edges of the platonic solids are Hamiltonian. We run the program for the graphs of the five platonic solids and show the first Hamiltonian circuit found by the algorithm in each case. For more details, input/output files and visualization see the demonstration program.

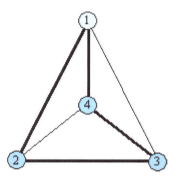

*Figure 7.1. Graph of the tetrahedron with a Hamiltonian circuit*

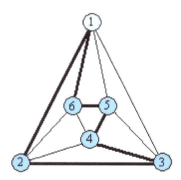

*Figure 7.2. Graph of the octahedron with a Hamiltonian circuit*

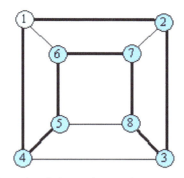

*Figure 7.3.* Graph of the cube with a Hamiltonian circuit

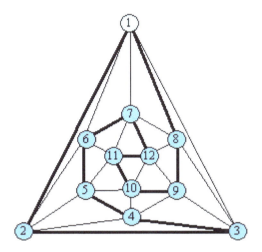

*Figure 7.4.* Graph of the icosahedron with a Hamiltonian circuit

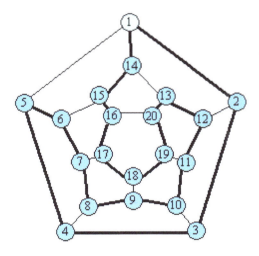

*Figure 7.5.* Graph of the dodecahedron with a Hamiltonian circuit

# 8.  *Dirac Graphs*

A simple graph $G$ with $n$ vertices that satisfies Dirac's conditions $n \geq 3$ and $\delta \geq n/2$ is called a *Dirac Graph*. By theorem 5.3, we know that the algorithm will always find a Hamiltonian circuit in a Dirac graph. We run the program for a small and a large Dirac graph, showing in each case the first Hamiltonian circuit found. For more details, input/output files and visualization, see the demonstration program.

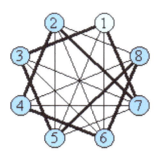

***Figure 8.1.*** *A small Dirac graph with a Hamiltonian circuit*

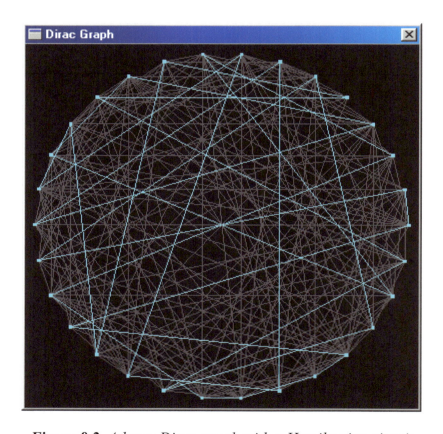

***Figure 8.2.*** *A large Dirac graph with a Hamiltonian circuit*

# 9. Knight's Tours

In 840 A.D., al-Adli [7], a renowned *shatranj* (chess) player of Baghdad is said to have discovered the first *re-entrant knight's tour*, a sequence of moves that takes the knight to each square on an $8 \times 8$ chessboard exactly once, returning to the original square. Many other re-entrant knight's tours were subsequently discovered but Euler [8] was the first mathematician to do a systematic analysis in 1766, not only for the $8 \times 8$ chessboard, but for re-entrant knight's tours on the general $n \times n$ chessboard. Given an $n \times n$ chessboard, define a *knight's graph* with a vertex corresponding to each square of the chessboard and an edge connecting vertex $i$ with vertex $j$ if and only if there is a legal knight's move from the square corresponding to vertex $i$ to the square corresponding to vertex $j$. Thus, a re-entrant knight's tour on the chessboard corresponds to a Hamiltonian circuit in the knight's graph. We run the program on the knight's graphs corresponding to chessboards of dimensions $8 \times 8$, $20 \times 20$, $40 \times 40$ and show the first re-entrant knight's tour found by the algorithm in each case. For more details, input/output files and visualization, see the demonstration program.

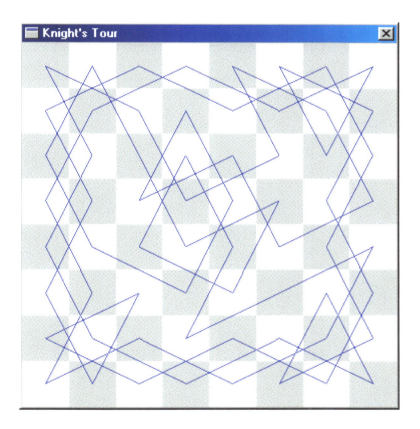

***Figure 9.1.*** *Re-entrant knight's tour on the* $8 \times 8$ *chessboard*

29

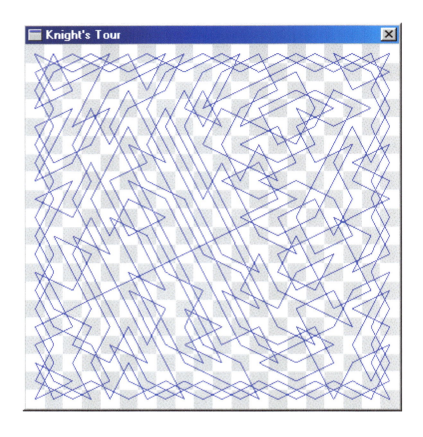

**Figure 9.2.** *Re-entrant knight's tour on the* $20 \times 20$ *chessboard*

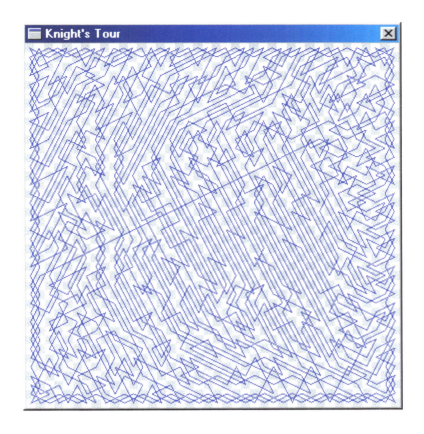

**Figure 9.3.** *Re-entrant knight's tour on the* $40 \times 40$ *chessboard*

# 10.  *References*

[1]  W. R. Hamilton, *Memorandum respecting a new System of Roots of Unity*, Philosophical Magazine, volume 12 (4th series), 1856.

[2]  G. A. Dirac, *Some theorems on abstract graphs*, Proc. London. Math. Soc. 2, 1952.

[3]  R. M. Karp, *Reducibility among combinatorial problems*, Complexity of Computer Computations, Plenum Press, 1972.

[4]  Stephen Cook, *The P versus NP Problem*, Official Problem Description, Millennium Problems, Clay Mathematics Institute, 2000.

[5]  J. A. Bondy and U.S.R. Murty , *Graph Theory with Applications*, North-Holland, 1976.

[6]  Stanley Lippman, *Essential C++*, Addison-Wesley, 2000.

[7]  H. J. R. Murray, *A History of Chess*, Oxford University Press, 1913.

[8]  L. Euler, *Solution d'une question curieuse qui ne paroit soumise a aucune analyse*, Mémoires de l'Académie Royale des Sciences et Belles Lettres de Berlin, Année 1759 15, 310-337, 1766.

[9]  Euclid, *Elements*, circa 300 B.C.

[10]  Plato, *Timaeaus*, circa 350 B.C.

*The Demonstration Program*

*http://www.dharwadker.org/hamilton*